LEARNING ABOUT THE EARTH

Coral Reefs

by Colleen Sexton

BELLWETHER MEDIA • MINNEAPOLIS, MN

Note to Librarians, Teachers, and Parents:

Blastoff! Readers are carefully developed by literacy experts and combine standards-based content with developmentally appropriate text.

Level 1 provides the most support through repetition of high-frequency words, light text, predictable sentence patterns, and strong visual support.

Level 2 offers early readers a bit more challenge through varied simple sentences, increased text load, and less repetition of high-frequency words.

Level 3 advances early-fluent readers toward fluency through increased text and concept load, less reliance on visuals, longer sentences, and more literary language.

Level 4 builds reading stamina by providing more text per page, increased use of punctuation, greater variation in sentence patterns, and increasingly challenging vocabulary.

Level 5 encourages children to move from "learning to read" to "reading to learn" by providing even more text, varied writing styles, and less familiar topics.

Whichever book is right for your reader, Blastoff! Readers are the perfect books to build confidence and encourage a love of reading that will last a lifetime!

This edition first published in 2009 by Bellwether Media.

No part of this publication may be reproduced in whole or in part without written permission of the publisher. For information regarding permission, write to Bellwether Media Inc., Attention: Permissions Department, Post Office Box 19349, Minneapolis, MN 55419.

Library of Congress Cataloging-in-Publication Data
Sexton, Colleen A., 1967–
  Coral reefs / by Colleen Sexton.
      p. cm. – (Blastoff! readers. Learning about the earth)
  Includes bibliographical references and index.
  Summary: "Simple text and full color photographs introduce beginning readers to the characteristics and geographical locations of coral reefs. Developed by literacy experts for students in kindergarten through third grade"—Provided by publisher.
  ISBN-13: 978-1-60014-228-4 (hardcover : alk. paper)
  ISBN-10: 1-60014-228-1 (hardcover : alk. paper)
  1. Coral reefs and islands–Juvenile literature. I. Title.

GB461.S44 2009
578.77'89–dc22   2008012254

Contents

A coral reef is an ocean
community that thousands
of plants and animals
call home.

TROPICS

EQUATOR

TROPICS

Coral reefs lie in water that is warm, shallow, and clear. Most coral reefs are in the **tropics**.

Small, tube-shaped animals called corals make up coral reefs.

Each coral makes a hard **skeleton** around the bottom of its body. The skeleton is left behind when the coral dies.

New corals attach their skeletons to the skeletons of dead corals. The skeletons make layers on top of each other.

The shells of clams, snails, and other animals mix in with the coral skeletons. They all become part of the reef.

Tiny living things called **algae** help the reef stick together.

Over time, the reef turns into
hard rock called **limestone**.

Coral reefs grow slowly.
Most grow about 5 inches
(13 centimeters) each year.
Some coral reefs have been
growing for millions of years.

The world's largest coral reef is the **Great Barrier Reef**. It stretches 1,250 miles (2,000 kilometers) along the coast of Australia.

fringing reef

Coral reefs grow in different forms. **Fringing reefs** grow outward from shore.

Barrier reefs grow offshore. A deep area of water lies between the shore and a barrier reef.

Some coral reefs are rings in the ocean. They once grew around islands. The islands have since sunk. These coral reefs are called **atolls**.

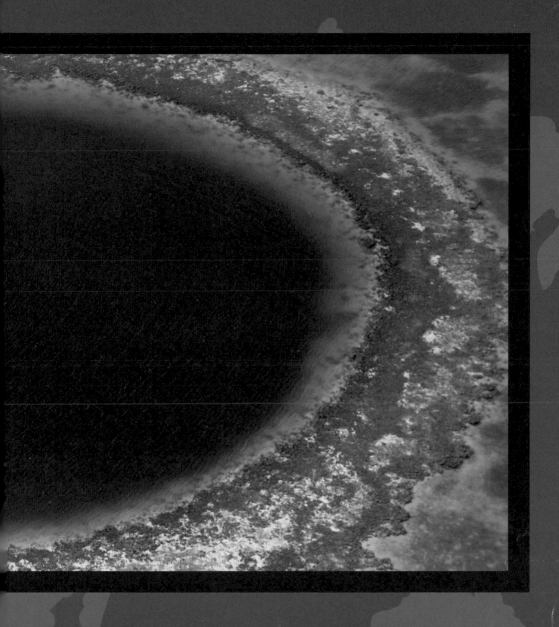

The top layer of a coral reef is alive. A reef can have billions of live corals.

Corals share the reef with other living things.

Seaweed and other types of algae may attach to a coral reef.

19

Fish of all shapes and sizes swim around coral reefs. A coral reef can have thousands of different kinds of fish.

Animals such as sharks, dolphins, sea turtles, and jellyfish visit coral reefs to find food. Coral reefs are beautiful and busy places!

Glossary

algae—living creatures that are like plants, but do not have roots or stems; most algae grow in water.

atoll—a coral reef shaped like a ring; an atoll is surrounded by open ocean.

barrier reef—an offshore coral reef that lies between land and the open ocean

fringing reef—a coral reef that grows outward from land

Great Barrier Reef—the world's largest coral reef

limestone—a rock made from the skeletons of corals and other dead animals

skeleton—a hard structure that supports and protects a body; corals that build reefs have a cup-shaped skeleton.

tropics—an area around the middle of the earth where the weather is always warm or hot

To Learn More

AT THE LIBRARY
Earle, Sylvia. *Coral Reefs*. Washington, D.C.:
National Geographic, 2003.

Moss, Miriam. *This Is the Reef*. London: Frances
Lincoln, 2007.

Silver, Donald M. *Coral Reef*. New York: Learning
Triangle Press, 1998.

ON THE WEB
Learning more about coral reefs
is as easy as 1, 2, 3.

1. Go to www.factsurfer.com

2. Enter "coral reefs" into search box.

3. Click the "Surf" button and you will see a list of
   related web sites.

With factsurfer.com, finding more information is just a
click away.

Index

The images in this book are reproduced through the courtesy of: Elisei Shafer, front cover; Sakis Papdopoulos / Getty Images, p. 4; Georgette Douwma / Getty Images, pp. 6, 10; Martin Strmko, p. 11; Mark Segal / Getty Images, p. 12; Martin Kers / Foto Natura / Getty Images, p. 15; Norbert Wu / Getty Images, pp. 16-17; Chris Newbert / Getty Images, pp. 18-19; Panoramic Images / Getty Images, pp. 20-21.